Table of Contents

Forward
Chapter 1   Why Escalation Management is Critical to Your Success
Chapter 2   The 7 Things B2B Customers Expect from Their Suppliers
Chapter 3   Prevention is Worth a Pound of Cure
Chapter 4   Understanding the Why
Chapter 5   Inspect What They Expect
Chapter 6   Implement Early Warning systems
Chapter 7   Equip and Empower the Front Line
Chapter 8   Coach Ownership - Eliminate Handoffs
Chapter 9   Support the Good Kind of Internal Escalations
Chapter 10 Assess and Prioritize Escalations
Chapter 11 The Escalation Conversation
Chapter 12 How to Gently Say "No" to Escalation Requests
Chapter 13 The Mediums for Your Messages
Chapter 14 Keeping the C Levels Informed
Chapter 15 How to Leverage Internal Escalation Paths
Chapter 16 The Importance of Follow-up
Chapter 17 Assess Your Escalation Management Approach
Appendix and Other Materials

Forward

The Blog Post That Started It All

Do you lead a customer support organization? Do you determine and implement customer experience strategy? Do you deliver projects or services on behalf of business customers? Then this handbook is for you! How do I know? Read on…

I have been blogging about customer operations, technical support and process improvement best practices for more than ten years in my external blog called "The Operations Blog" and as a guest blogger on other websites.

Back in April 2016, I published a blog post called "10 Tips To Master Customer Escalation Management". At first it got what I would call normal readership with about 700 views per month. But, then something crazy happened. In 2018 it went viral, and began to get close to 3,000 views per month, a 300 percent increase. Also, this level of interest has continued into 2020. Wow!

Most of these blog visitors landed on the site after using a search engine like Google or Bing. They put in search phrases like, "client escalation management", "how to avoid supervisor calls", "better way to handle escalations" or "how to reduce escalations". In answer to this increasing demand, this book is for you.

If You Support Customers, You Have Customer Escalations

For the majority of my career I have been leading customer-facing service organizations. When you provide a product or service, there will always be some customers who are not satisfied, and a subset of those customers will escalate to the leadership team for help. Through these experiences and the input from other customer operations experts, I have compiled what I believe are the critical best practices to successfully handling these escalations.

Effectively managing customer escalations can have a direct and positive impact on customer retention, customer loyalty and the likelihood a customer will recommend your business. Many CX experts predict that customer experience will overtake price and product quality as the key brand differentiator. I hope you enjoy this handbook!

Chapter 1

Why Escalation Management is Critical to Your Success

"Sorry As a Service", is Real!

You have likely heard of the acronym SaaS which stands for software as a service. But, have you heard of a different SaaS that stands for sorry as a service?

Yes, there is actually a growing business in the UK called Sorry As A Service which enables companies to quickly and automatically send out personal gifts to customers who had service issues, with the intent to win them back. Service issues have become so common, we need other businesses in place to help apologize for the mistakes. Wow! (By the way, "Sorry as a Service" is pretty cool. Check out their website at https://sorryasaservice.com.)

Customer service mistakes lead to customer service escalations. And, effectively managing these escalations is a topic on many leaders' minds.

Recently, I had breakfast with a colleague who is a vice president of technical support for a large, publicly traded software company. I noticed right away that she seemed very stressed out. As we discussed the reasons why, she said that she was spending all of her time on customer escalations. This was taking her away from running the department or doing anything strategic. Because she had to support global customers, she was on the phone morning and night. Not only was it a time issue, it was also impacting her job satisfaction. Managing escalations is exhausting!

Fast-forward a few weeks later, I was chatting with a vice president of customer delivery for a different enterprise software firm, and she also brought up escalations. In fact she was looking to hire someone to run the day-to-day operations so she had more time to handle the important escalations.

Customer escalations take a lot of time. They can be upsetting and stressful. They can be very difficult to defuse and address. And they can be tricky to decrease and prevent.

Conversely, customer escalations can be a good thing. They provide opportunities for us to learn how we can improve our product or services. Also, if handled well, these moments of truth can actually improve our customers' perceptions of us and increase customer loyalty.

There have been a number of studies undertaken that looked at three categories of customers: 1) customers with no problems with their suppliers, 2) customers with a problem that was NOT handled to their satisfaction, and 3) customers with a problem that was handled well and met their expectations.

In every study, the customers who had a problem that was handled well, spent more over time, were more loyal and were more likely to recommend that supplier. There are also many studies that link improvements to customer retention to improvements in business profits.

You have the ability to make a major impact on people and profitability, by effectively managing customer escalations.

Complaints versus Escalations

This book focuses on managing customer escalations not customer complaints. A customer complaint is defined as an expression of dissatisfaction that is made from a customer to the party responsible. (Landon, 1980) A customer escalation is a scenario where a customer is dissatisfied and asks to speak to an employee at a higher level within an organization to listen and/or to resolve the issue. A complaint is a predecessor of an escalation.

Business to Business (B2B) versus Business to Consumer (B2C) Escalations

Much has been written about consumer customer experiences with online retailers, cable companies, airlines etc. It is important to know that there are very big differences in customer needs and the delivery of customer operations for businesses versus consumers, and therefore differences in how we should manage escalations. Here are some specific examples.

B2B customers start out less satisfied. According to McKinsey research, B2B customer experience index ratings rank far lower than their B2C counterparts, with the average B2B company scoring below 50 percent compared to the typical 65 to 85 percent scored for B2C companies. (This is against a range of 1 to 100 percent.)

B2C sales are typically a standard, repeatable product offering, and as a result, easier to deploy and service. B2B offerings tend to be more customized, and therefore more complex.

With B2B, service failures not only impact the business customer (i.e. your customer), but may also impact their end customers or consumers. Here is an example.

I am shopping at a large retailer and my shopping cart is full. I go to the cashier ready to make my $500 purchase using a credit card. The clerk shares that the credit card point-of-sale device is down, and she can only accept checks and cash.

She has called the credit card device provider (the B2B relationship) but they have not fixed the issue yet. I have no cash and left my check book at home so I leave very frustrated and the store loses my $500 sale. The B2B customer, i.e. the store, experienced a loss. And, I, the consumer, posts bad reviews on social media and never shops there again. A double whammy!

B2C transactions generally have one or two key decision-makers while B2B have multiple. These may include stakeholders and/ or users from technical to legal to purchasing to C-level. Also, a single B2B customer may be spread over multiple locations or geographies. When you are resolving a B2B escalation, it may take longer and require more touch-points.

In many organizations, about 20 percent of the business customers account for about 80% of the revenue or profit. An individual customer relationship could be worth thousands or millions per year. Business customers are not created equal, so a cookie cutter approach to escalation management will not work.

Being Human-The Link Between B2B and B2C

Although there are differences when interacting with business and consumer customers, there is one thing that is exactly the same. That is, we are working with human beings. Human beings are complex, not always logical, and every human is unique. In addition, emotions will always be involved in any type of escalation conversation.

Per Forrester, the global research experts, ease, effectiveness, and emotion all contribute to a positive customer experience, but companies often focus too narrowly on effectiveness. If we master the emotional connection, it will have the biggest impact on improving a customer's experience, increasing their loyalty and enhancing their perception of our brand in the marketplace.

Identifying these emotions can be very difficult, but ultimately relies on us listening to what customers say they feel, observing body language and observing other physical cues. Through these techniques, we can attempt to discern if a customer is happy, dissatisfied or somewhere in between. And then, we can adjust our responses accordingly.

In its 2019, "ROI of Customer Experience study", the Qualtrics XM Institute reported on the correlation between elements of the customer experience and customer loyalty. The study analyzed three key levers that drive customer experience. These were success, effort, and emotion. Of these three, emotion had the biggest and positive impact on a customer's likelihood to purchase more, recommend a company and forgive a bad experience.

Effectively Managing B2B Escalations

The focus of this book is Business to Business (B2B) escalation management. It covers how suppliers, B2B customer service providers or support leaders can effectively handle escalations from business enterprises. These escalations may happen any time during the customer lifecycle starting during pre-sales, to contracting, through implementation/onboarding and then to ongoing support and relationship development.

Your first priority as a supplier, B2B customer service provider or support leader is to prevent un-needed escalations from occurring. When this is not possible, there are best practices to follow to successfully manage customer escalations.

Here are my tips to master customer escalation management and to achieve the best outcomes for your customers, your employees and your business.

The handbook will cover escalation prevention, escalation response and internal escalation paths.

Chapter 2

The 7 Things B2B Customers Expect from Their Suppliers

To effectively manage escalations, it is critical that any business service provider understands what B2B customers expect from their suppliers overall, from a customer experience perspective.

I pooled my combined research from industry experts like KPMG, B2B International, Salesforce and Oracle, talked with renowned customer experience experts, and considered 20 years of my own CX experiences. This resulted in the following list of seven standards that B2B customers demand from their suppliers:

1) Understand THEIR business: B2B customers expect you to listen, understand who they are, what their business does and to tailor communications and experiences to their unique needs. They also expect that you will act with empathy during any business discussion.

2) Understand OUR business: B2B customers expect suppliers to demonstrate deep credibility and competency in the products and services that they sell and support.

3) Be proactive: B2B customers expect suppliers to anticipate customer needs and strive to resolve issues BEFORE they occur.

4) Consistently deliver: B2B suppliers must deliver on contractual expectations.

5) Be responsive: B2B suppliers must act with urgency to answer questions and resolve problems quickly and accurately.

6) Continuously adapt and improve: B2B providers must demonstrate flexibility and willingness to change, especially based on feedback from B2B customers. They must continually maximize value and minimize customer efforts, in the delivery of products and services.

7) Throughout all of these steps and processes, suppliers must keep customers informed of what happened, what is happening and what's next. In other words, communicate, communicate, communicate.

If all goes well with items 1 through 7, most business customers will view their supplier as "easy to do business with" which is a major accomplishment for a B2B firm. Keep these standards in mind, as you put together your customer escalation improvement plans.

Chapter 3

Prevention is Worth a Pound of Cure

Ben Franklin (scientist, inventor, politician) once said, "An ounce of prevention is worth a pound of cure". I think he should have been in customer support!

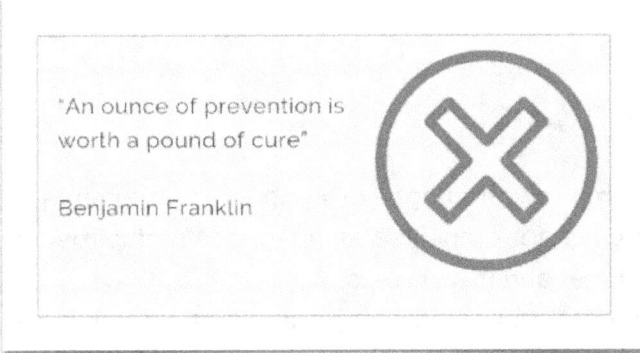

Your first priority as a customer service provider or support leader is to prevent un-needed escalations from occurring. Why is this important?

It is important because escalations can have a major impact on your business results. Escalations, when not managed properly, can permanently damage your customer relationships, lead to customer and revenue attrition, and negatively impact your brand in the marketplace. This can lead to future lost sales.

Customers Will Walk - Maybe Run

In his December 2019 blog post, "Customer Service and CX Predictions for 2020" customer experience expert Shep Hyken talked about expected changes in customer behavior. One of these predictions is that since customers are smarter about service, they will walk away faster if a company provides a bad experience.

A recent study by Gladly, a customer service technology provider, further confirmed Shep's prediction. Its study showed that 84% of customers will switch to a competitor after three poor customer experiences, and 17% will switch after just one poor experience.

A 2013 independent study about B2C and B2B Customer Service completed by Dimensional Research and sponsored by Zendesk had some interesting findings. The most common reaction to bad service among B2B buyers, was simply to stop buying from that company. Conversely, good customer interactions led to an increase in future B2B sales.

Escalations Have a Cost

Customer escalations cost money and negatively impact your company's bottom line. This includes costs for employee salaries, contractual penalties if service levels are not met and travel costs.

Large volumes of customer escalations can destroy employee morale. We would all prefer to spend our time on engaging, value add activities. Talking to upset customers all day steals resources away from strategic projects, ignites attrition and squashes innovation.

Chapter 4

Understanding The Why

Understand Why Escalations Occur

Customer escalations, although challenging and stressful, are also great learning opportunities. By understanding why customers escalate and are dissatisfied, you can work to improve the end to end customer experience for all of your customers.

To uncover the root causes for escalations, gather information from multiple sources. Review the most common reasons customers contact your support organization. Review the types of problems that take the longest to resolve. Read comments in customer feedback surveys. Talk to customers who have recently made an escalation. Ask your front line support, sales and engineering staff members for feedback. By compiling multiple sources of data and advice, trends will emerge.

Once you understand the why behind customer escalations, you can create and implement an action plan to address these critical problems.

It is common to find that the causes of dissatisfaction will fall into these high level categories: people, products/offerings, technology and processes. Customer also value communication, responsiveness, commitment, and proactivity.

Michael Pace, a well known expert and consultant in the area of customer experience, shared that customer escalations primarily stem from a process issue and/or an expectation cause. Process issues may include product defects, service failures, fraud incidents, or process exceptions. Expectation causes relate to poor communication between the supplier and the customer. This miscommunication can be verbal, written, heard, or implied. Many times escalations are both a process and expectation created issue.

Impact Communications Incorporated, a phone and communication skills training company, published a study on why customers escalate phone calls in a call center environment.

They found seven reasons: 1) agent lack of knowledge, 2) being told no without any apparent reason or explanation, 3) the agent lacking confidence, 4) the agent having a negative or disagreeable attitude, 5) not receiving an apology, 6) the agent not communicating clearly and 7) the agent not adapting to the pace of the customer. Do any of these sound familiar?

The Link Between Timing & Causes

It's also important to understand the timing of your customer escalations. Are customers usually upset before they contact you? Do they become upset while interacting with your staff members or self service websites? Do they become upset after the interaction is over? Link the timing of the dissatisfaction with your root cause information, to create the most impactful plans to minimize customer escalations.

No Bandaids!

I strongly recommend that you avoid "quick fixes" to address root causes of customer escalations. There is often a desire (maybe pressure from the customer or senior leadership) to achieve quick wins when solving complex problems. This may work on occasion, but there is nothing worse than telling a customer that a problem has been fixed and then having that same problem recur a few weeks later.

Again, once you understand the root cause(s) of customer escalations, you can create and implement an action plan to address these critical problems.

Chapter 5

Inspect What They Expect

A few years ago I completed an analysis on software project implementation times. We had received a number of escalations from customers who were unhappy with the quality, schedule and cost of their projects. The hypothesis at the time was as follows: if we just implement faster, customers will be happier. Further, the biggest opportunity to shorten the time frame of the projects was in the control of the project and technical teams working on the implementation.

A thorough review was completed of not just the project lifecycle, but all of the steps leading up to it including the sales cycle, the contracting cycle, and the high level requirements cycle.

In the end, we found that the key levers to reduce the implementation time were actually very different. It was not a work harder and faster opportunity. Instead, the opportunity to improve was tied to customer expectation setting. This happened pre-project, when the salesperson was negotiating with the customer. We also learned that customers do not always want speed, instead they want predictability and clear schedules.

Our key takeaway was: If we did a better job to define, document and agree upon customer expectations up front, they will be more satisfied later in the process. This will reduce escalations during the project lifecycle.

These learnings apply to many different processes and problems. When looking at the causes of escalations, we often focus on the process right in front of us, not the steps leading up to it or after it. A lot of business customer expectation setting happens during the sales cycles, during the marketing cycles, in product management brochures, in face to face meetings and in casual discussions.

Our key takeaway was:

If we did a better job to define, document and agree upon customer expectations up front, they will be more satisfied later in the process. This will reduce escalations during the project lifecycle.

The Ritz Carlton hotel chain known for industry leading customer service, recently shared its philosophies on the do's and don'ts of customer expectation setting. The company recommended that businesses deliver on committed time frames and practice seamless communication. Per the Ritz, it is important not to oversell products and services and ensure you can deliver on your promises. If businesses set realistic expectations they can prevent future disappointments.

In her 2020 article titled, "9 Real World Examples of Setting Clear Expectations with Your Customers", Sarah Chambers shared some interesting perspectives. Per Sarah, "If we don't provide our customer reference points by setting customer expectations, customers will search out their own reference points. That might be your competitors' service or past experience they had.

Their evaluation becomes much easier when we set expectations around the service we provide. This gives customers a simple starting point to compare their actual experience. If we meet or exceed their expectations – they'll think the service was great!" Great points.

In summary, if you and your company do a great job setting customer expectations up front and ongoing, you will have fewer customer escalations to manage. The company does far more damage to its trust and reputation by agreeing to provide a service that cannot be delivered. Instead, make promises that are realistic and achievable, and then go the distance to over-deliver on the promise. Under promise and over deliver.

Chapter 6

Implement Early Warning Systems

A customer experience early warning system, is a system that detects and then notifies targeted company personnel when something bad is likely to happen. In the context of this book, that bad thing is an escalation.

In order to identify a future "at risk" customer, you need to understand what a happy or normal customer behaves like. To do this, identify the factors that measure customer behavior for your unique business type. For example, these may include the number of transactions processed, the number of new users added per month, the number of emails sent, revenue spent per year, number of logins per month, number of service tickets opened or average speed to pay invoices.

Once you understand what the norm looks like, your early warning system can identify deviations from that norm. Here are some examples.

Deviations For Specific Customers

- If a customer who spends over $4,500 per year, opens more than 2 customer support tickets in a month, they will be very unhappy and es-

calate. Because you know this, at the moment that the customer opens that third support ticket, your early warning system should send a notification.
- If one of your top 10 customers experiences any type of unplanned outage with their SaaS product, they will be vey unhappy and escalate.
- If a customer who normally pays their invoices on time, suddenly does not pay their invoice on time, after an appropriate number of days notify internal personnel.

Deviations For Groups of Customers

- Large spike or large drop in call volume or tickets.
- Unusually long wait times or problem resolution times.
- Unusually high or low transaction volume flowing through customer cloud offerings.

Early Warning System Tools

An early warning detection system can be built in several different ways. In its most basic form, you could leverage your marketing, ops or finance team and have them pull data manually from your key systems, cross-reference information and then build models to manually identify your trends and exceptions. There are also external companies who can help you build these models leveraging data scientists. This process is called CX predictive analytics.

Many of the newer customer relationship management (CRM), marketing automation or ticketing systems have these capabilities built right in. The software automatically does the required analysis and then can run reports or alert key personnel via a system prompt, email or text, when action is needed.

For example, Totango CRM offers a four component early warning system. The components are sensors, event detection, decision support and customer engagement. The tool monitors data, is able to detect meaningful customer events, and then assist leadership to take the appropriate actions.

If your focus is primarily a call center environment and you record phone calls, there are software products (e.g. NICE, Calibrio, Verint) that can listen to the conversations and detect future escalations. They do this by listening for certain words, phrases and in some cases, voice inflection.

Action Leads to Prevention

Identifying these problems is not enough. You must act in order to prevent an escalation from occurring. For each type of problem or exception, identify a path that makes sense for your business.

An action could include things like a proactive call, a proactive email or even a proactive visit with a customer or group of customers. It should be clear who owns each type of action. Some actions can be completed by front line service experts. Others may require a touch from a senior executive.

I have found that even if a customer has a difficult problem, a proactive, timely contact by the right person can turn a problem into a relationship building opportunity. Others agree. In his article, " 5 ways to turn your unhappy customer into a valuable resource", Neil Patel, a world renowned marketing guru and online influencer, shared, "Each dissatisfied contact has the potential for becoming your company's best advertisement, a key referral source, and a stealth undercover operative – if you are willing to listen.

Going out of your way to accommodate a customer's needs makes them feel important, respected and in control. An unhappy customer that's transformed into a delighted one becomes even more loyal than a satisfied customer. In other words, we are even more satisfied when we've had a problem and it's been satisfactorily handled than if we never had the problem to begin with." Great tips Neil!

Taking This a Step Further...

Customer support providers must begin to think of their top priority as incident prevention not incident management.

Incident management focuses on reacting to customer demand (incidents, tickets, questions) and solving problems. It's about reducing case aging, reducing backlog, achieving service levels and achieving case closure SLAs. These behaviors can result in an environment of fire fighting.

Incident prevention focuses on activities that will reduce or eliminate a customer's need to contact you. It is about identifying and eliminating problems before customers know they are there. It is about working upstream, not at the end of a process.

This is such an important concept, I want to plant the seed among our discussion about escalations. Fewer incidents means fewer escalations. Fewer incidents will improve your customer experience, save money and improve your top and bottom line.

Back to escalations....

Chapter 7

Equip, Trust and Empower the Front Line

To prevent escalations, we must equip, trust and empower the front line employees to provide an experience that meets your customers' expectations and delivers on contractual agreements.

This means ensuring that the team members interacting directly with customers have the tools and training that they need to be successful. This includes new employee training and ongoing refresher training. Depending on the complexity of issues, checklists or quick reference guides may be helpful. Also, more and more companies are creating valuable, online knowledge bases for use by both employees and customers to find answers to the most common questions or problems.

The staff members interacting directly with customers must also be empowered to use their judgment and make the majority of day to day decisions on behalf of their customers. If the most common and most important decisions always require supervisor, manager or other approvals, that demonstrates lack or trust and is a red flag. Only exceptions, should require multi-level approval.

This seems like it should be simple, but it is not. Many leaders stay too involved in the day to day decisions and micro-manage their team members. If employees don't feel that their leadership team trusts them, they likely will not trust their leadership, which creates an unhappy work environment. In addition, when leaders stay too involved in day to day activities, they do not have enough time for the strategic activities. Bottom line, treat your employees the way you would want to be treated. Trust them to do the right things.

Finally, responsibilities, accountabilities and measurements of success among any customer facing team must be clear and documented. For example, if front line staff members are measured on sales only, or on speed of interactions neither measurement will drive a positive customer experience. Job expectations must align with the type of customer experience you are attempting to create.

Chapter 8

Coach Ownership - Eliminate Handoffs

Coach team members to take ownership of difficult customer situations and avoid passing them off to someone else whenever possible.

I have found that there is always "something" you can do to help a customer. This may include simply listening, offering your name and contact number, reaching out to someone else on their behalf, asking additional questions, sending them some related documentation or going out of your way to find the right answers to their questions or concerns.

When a customer asks one of your team members to help them escalate an issue, instead of agreeing, coach your team to use scripting to keep ownership of the situation. For example:

"Susan, I understand your frustration with the project and I am also concerned about our ability to hit the upcoming dates. I do have a suggestion. Before we escalate to a Vice President, can I take the time to engage some of our senior engineers who have not been involved to this point, to get a fresh perspective? They are more likely to get us back on track, then engaging a senior leader at this point."

Even if it is not in an employee's job description and/ or an employee may not have the specific training to get something done, at times he or she may need to be a buffer. This means that to the customer, there is a single point of contact. Behind the scenes, there may be a number of staffers working together to solve the problem.

I believe that every customer related process handoff is a detractor from our ability to provide a positive customer experience.

Handle the Handoffs!

In addition to equipping and empowering customer facing staff members, companies can reduce handoffs by automating systems and processes. When a system is automated, no human intervention is needed to make something happen, which can add time and reduce quality.

Better access to information will also help. We sometimes shy away from allowing employees to access all the systems and data necessary to do their roles, due to regulatory, audit or information security reasons.

Lack of access can also be the result of lack of trust. Sometimes these considerations are valid, and sometimes they should be questioned. If lack of access is materially impacting speed, quality or customer satisfaction, we should question the status quo and see what alternatives are available.

Chapter 9

Support the Good Kind of Internal Escalations

Create an environment where employees are not afraid to ask for help, and leverage the "good" kind of escalations. Wait.. are there good escalations? Yes there are!

If you work in a customer facing environment such as technical support, customer care or implementation services, challenges will always occur at some point in a customer's lifecycle. When these challenges occur, we have an opportunity to turn a challenge into a positive experience for both the employees and customers, by simply asking for help. This may mean asking for help from a peer, a boss or even a subject matter expert in another department.

Unfortunately, I have observed that employees tend to hesitate before asking for assistance. They wait to escalate internally, until the problem has gotten significantly worse and we have little time to react.

Encourage employees to ask for help early in the remediation process and before the problem becomes a full fledged crisis. If they escalate before an important date has passed or a service level agreement (SLA) is missed, we still have a chance to meet the customers' commitments.

The better we work collectively and proactively to identify options and a resolution, we will eliminate the need for a customer to escalate higher within a company.

Link Between Employee Experience and Customer Experience

For my own personal development, I follow a number of customer experience thought leaders by attending seminars, watching webinars and reading relevant blogs. One of my favorite thought leaders is Bruce Temkin @btemkin, who often posts in one of my favorite blogs, The CX Matters blog by Qualtrics.

Bruce Temkin and his team have completed a number of studies on the link between engaged employees and the delivery of a quality customer experience. They have found that companies who inform, inspire, instruct, involve and incent employees in the right ways, have higher levels of employee engagement and morale. Also, there is a direct and positive link between engaged employees and engaged customers.

Per Temkin, "Unengaged employees don't create engaged customers. If you want to differentiate your customer experience, then improve your relationship with employees."

I have personally planned, led and executed a significant number of employee engagement improvement initiatives over the years. And, I have seen the direct link between engaged employees and overall business results, not just customer experience.

In order to better manager or eliminate customer escalations we must improve the overall customer experience. In order to improve the overall customer experience, we must also focus on improving employee engagement.

As mentioned earlier, if employees have to handle fewer upset customers, this will have a positive impact on their job satisfaction. Escalations are stressful to handle. It is difficult to spend minutes or hours having to listen to upset customers and/or to apologize over and over for shortcomings. There are also times when customers may yell or use obscenities during escalations. If customer service providers spend too much time on escalations, it will take a toll on employee engagement and morale.

Chapter 10

Assess and Prioritize Escalations

We are now going to shift our focus to managing escalations.

The very first step in an effective escalation management program is to assess and prioritize before taking any action. Not all customers are created equal. Not all escalations are created equal. There are only so many hours in a day and a finite number of human resources in your company, so we must invest wisely. Therefore, pause and assess before you begin the escalation response process.

Know Your Most Important Customers

It is an important best practice to agree on, document and communicate a list of your most important customers. Why? So employees in your company can recognize these names, and can handle them with special care.

Creating this list may sound easy, but it is usually more complicated than it seems. If you ask a salesperson, they will likely tell you that all of his or her customers are the most important. Your finance team may recommend to prioritize the list based on which customers are most profitable. Your executive team may be most concerned with the highest revenue generators and those with the greatest chance of growth in the next 12 months.

As previously mentioned, in many B2B organizations about 20% of the business customers account for about 80% of the revenue or profit. Therefore, an individual customer relationship could be worth thousands or millions per year. Wow!

Without the list in place, you risk dropping the ball with one of the most important customers and spending too much time with a client who is less strategic. Interestingly, it is often the smaller, less strategic customers who create the most noise and demand more of our time, while, our larger, most important customers can be quiet until something is really wrong.

It is worth the time and effort to put together a cross-functional team to define the top customer criteria and manage it on an ongoing basis.

Accessibility

Once you have agreed on the criteria and documented your list of top customers, it must be easily accessible to the employees who need it, in a shared space online, like a CRM (customer relationship management) system.

There should also be a cadence in place to update this list, at minimum, on a quarterly basis. (Hint: Keep in mind that this top customer list would be very valuable to your competitors, so it should only be accessible on a "need to know" basis and clearly marked Sensitive and Company Confidential.)

Understand Which Problems Qualify for Escalation

Assessing the urgency of an escalation request is both an art and a science, and it requires a bit of detective work.

There are some customers who escalate every time they have a request, and others who only escalate when it is truly warranted. In addition, you will get escalations through third parties like account executives or resellers. Because they tend to be further away from the day to day operations, they may not have the knowledge to truly assess the criticality of a situation.

When you receive an escalation request directly or indirectly, I recommend that you first check your CRM (customer relationship management) system, and review the customer's account activity history. Also, talk to the team members who are working directly with this customer. This will help you understand whether the issue is new, or something that they have experienced multiple times. This will also help put the issue in context with other activities the customer may be involved in such as a pending new deal, a product implementation or migration.

After you leverage your tools, begin an escalation conversation with the customer and ask lots of open ended questions. For example: Can you tell me a bit more about what happened? When did the problem first occur. How did you identify the issue? How is this problem impacting your business? Is the problem still happening?

Once you have gathered some baseline information, you can determine the right approach and decide which staff members you will involve.

Chapter 11

The Escalation Conversation

A High Level Conversation Template

A leader or service provider's key goals during any escalation interaction are to first listen and understand, and then to re-instill confidence and re-build trust with the customer. This does not mean you need to have all the answers or the perfect script. Try these five steps for the first conversation.

1. Listen to the customer. Ask questions. Listen some more.
   - Allow the customer time to share everything they want to. Let them vent.
2. Acknowledge that you heard and understand what the customer is concerned about.
3. Recommend some next steps or options. If possible give the customer a choice, so they feel in control.
4. Thank the customer for their business. Reinforce how important the relationship is.
5. Schedule a follow up interaction.

During the conversation, demonstrate concern, empathy and urgency. At the same time, remain calm and avoid being defensive.

Calm.. Your Super Power

In addition to my work experience in customer operations, I also teach yoga. As a yoga instructor, I attempt to create an environment where my students can quiet their minds and relax. Depending on the class, I use different techniques such as playing soothing music, sharing essential oils, using breathing techniques, or using a soft, calming voice. I also attempt to project confidence and knowledge of the practice I am teaching. My behavior and the energy I create in the class have a direct impact on how the students feel in my class.

These same concepts hold true in customer escalation discussions. I do not recommend playing yoga music or passing around essential oils, LOL, but calmness can be your superpower.

In a tense customer escalation conversation, if you behave in a calm manner, others will likely begin to mirror you. Staying calm can help the customer gain perspective about the situation. Staying calm can help instill confidence. When all parties are calm, you are in a much better position to discuss next steps and the resolution options.

If you are in a face to face scenario, also be conscious of your body language. In addition to projecting calm, be sure to retain eye contact, elongate your spine (oops, yoga teacher talk), sit or stand up straight and allow your arms to rest by your sides. Your body language should match your verbal queues.

Avoid Being Defensive

A friend of mine owns her own home improvement business and she recently called me for some advice about an escalation. She had installed carpet at a customer's site and the customer was not happy with it. She made several attempts to correct the situation and went above and beyond working with the manufacturer to replace some areas of concern.

The next week the customer sent her an escalation email and demanded a large refund on the carpet.

My friend had written a draft email response immediately and read it to me on the phone. When I heard it, I cringed. In short, the first few lines were all about how the customer was wrong, and how my friend's team, had done everything right. In fact, it went into great detail, point by point, about how right she was!

After helping my friend calm down (it's only carpet!), I recommended a few things. First, one should not send an email response while upset. Second, remove the defensive tone from the email. I advised that being defensive and trying to prove that she was right, would not help resolve the situation. In fact, it could actually make it worse.

In the end she considered my advice, waited a few days and ultimately mailed the customer a thank you letter and small gift. She has not heard back from that customer and the refund request has been put to bed.

When you are working with a customer on an escalation if you react with defensiveness and focus on why the company is right and/or why the customer is wrong, it will only make things worse. The customer will sense your feelings, and that will increase his or her own level of emotion which makes the conversation more difficult. Instead, stay calm and focus on listening to understand the customer's position.

I once had a boss who, when faced with feedback or information he was not expecting, would acknowledge and summarize the feedback and then say, "I need some time to process this.". I really like this approach for certain types of escalations, as the feedback giver feels heard and validated, while the listener has time to think through next steps.

The Right Words Matter

I was recently listening in to a customer escalation conference call and I was very concerned at how a few employees were responding to the customer's questions. Instead of using words to instill trust, calm and credibility, they used "wishy washy" language that actually caused more doubt and escalated the customer's feeling of pain. In addition, the employees made mention of other departments and did not take ownership of the issues at hand.

When dealing with a customer escalation, the words you use are critical to improve the likelihood of a successful outcome.

A few years ago, I discovered Jack Griffin's book, "How to Say It: Creating Complete Customer Satisfaction" and have summarized a few language tips from Griffin that directly apply to this topic. You can include some or all of these in escalation interactions with customers.

Words of Calm: We'll resolve this. I'm listening. Full support. Satisfy. Let's do this together. Take all the time that you need.

Words of Apology: My error/mistake. Assure. Accommodate. Take comments like yours very seriously. Whatever is necessary.

Words of Helping: Advice, aid, assist. Everything you need. Correct this. I will fix it. We'll expedite it. Urgent. Under control.

Words of Credibility: Believe. Certainty. Competence. Ethical. Absolute. I am confident. You have my word. I recommend.

There are also words and phrases to AVOID using in escalation interactions. These include: Our policy. Not our fault. Not something we cover. This has never happened before. I can't. I'm pretty sure. No.

Avoid Department Name Dropping

One of my personal pet peeves during escalation conversations is department name dropping. This is the practice of naming other departments and blaming them for the customer's problems.

Here is an example of this negative behavior. "I am sorry the problem has taken so long to fix. The ticket sat in our engineering organization for three weeks. Then the ticket got sent to our Q/A area. We finally agreed on a fix, but engineering can not schedule the code drop for another month."

Pointing fingers at other departments, even if the information is true, will only make customers more angry and will actually delay solving the problem.

Here is how that employee could share a similar message in a way that instills confidence and credibility. "I am sorry the problem has taken so long to fix. Due to the complexity of the problem, I engaged our top technical lead who has deep expertise in your product. She completed a number of assessments to understand the cause and recently found the solution. We have scheduled the fix to drop in our very next release, which is early next month."

Less is More

Sometimes it is better to say less than more. You may know that either you or a colleague dropped the ball on something. You may know that the product has a history of malfunctioning at certain times similar to what the customer has been experiencing. But, you do not need to tell the customer this. There is sometimes a fine line between being honest, communicating, and over sharing.

During customer conversations (really, any conversation) simplify your language, avoid acronyms and favor more common technical phrases. When you need to use technical terms, use those that are more commonly understood. For example, say "memory" instead of "RAM". If you must use a complex technical term, also define what the term means. For example, "The RGF database malfunctioned. This is the database where we store transaction histories."

The most successful customer conversations are clear, easy to understand and concentrate on what you can do to solve the customer's problems. This approach helps to refocus your customer's attention on what's next.

Provide Perspective and Context

In escalation conversations, there are two additional elements that can be very important to include, at the right time in the right way. These help focus the customer on the big picture and the future relationship.

First, put the problem or failure in context to the bigger picture of what services have been delivered to this customer. Some examples are, a single missed SLA over a 2 year period, a single product defect during a lengthy project implementation with 10 code releases, a 10 minute outage after 12 months with 99.999% up time. It is important to present this information in a non-defensive way. Second, focus on the long term strategy to improve the customer's experience. Here is an example of what this conversation might sound like.

"Tom, I really appreciate your partnership over the past month as we worked together on the system issue. Since we put the permanent fix in place three weeks ago, your end to end network has been stable and transaction processing speed has actually improved by 15 percent. I thought it would be helpful to provide a visual of your system's up time and transaction processing trends over the past two years. (Refer to charts.) With the exception of last month's service failures, speed and availability have been consistently strong.

I also put together a quick list of some of the actions we are taking to further update the network, and increase processing speeds. We are expecting that you and your end customers will notice some continual improvements in service month over month for the rest of this year."

Chapter 12

How to Gently Say "No" to Escalation Requests

Because all customers are not created equal (refer back to Chapter 10), and we have finite time, money and resources, there will be occasions when we must gently say "no" and provide other options to an escalation request. There are also occasions, when we simply need more time before responding.

Remember that any time you say yes, you are also saying no to something or someone else. Conversely, any time you say no, you free up the same time and resources for something more strategic, more critical or more impactful.

Escalation Categories

As mentioned in previous chapters, business escalation requests tend to fall into three categories: time, money or people.

Time demands: This is a request for something to be completed or fixed by a certain date. This could happen because your product or service is so critical to their day to day operations, they can not live without it (e.g. payroll, payments, security). It could be a case where your end customer has other projects in play, and your company's deliverable must happen first. Or, (quite common) your business contact made promises to upper management that a task would be delivered by a certain date, and their reputation is on the line, if it is not completed.

Cost demands: This is a request for a discount or refund. We work in a time when business leaders are consistently asked to do more with less. Budgets are constantly being trimmed. Dollars are often reallocated to other projects during the year. If a customer is asking for a refund or a discount, find out what prompted the request and whether you believe it is reasonable or your are contractually obligated to take action.

People demands: This is a request to work with a named employee or an executive leader on a specific deliverable. In every company where I have worked there are key, go-to employees for different products or services. These are the superstars who are incredibly easy to work with and/or who have deep expertise in their domain area. It is common for customers to know who they are and ask to work with them directly. There is also a perception by customers that if a VP, SVP, EVP or C level leader is involved, their problems will be solved faster.

Here are some scripting examples for escalation requests and how you can gently respond in a way that says no and provides alternatives.

Common Request	Gentle "No" Or More Time Response
We need to meet immediately about this problem.	I completely understand the urgency of the situation. Before we meet, I want to make sure we are prepared to answer your questions and have the right people involved. Can we schedule a call in two hours?
This problem must be fixed by tomorrow.	Yes, we have all of our top people working on this issue and our focus is resolving it as soon as possible. It is a very complex issue, that not only requires people, but also a code fix. Are there other activities happening at your company that are impacted by this fix timeline? Is the work-around sufficient for the next few days?
I want X to come on site to fix this.	I agree that X is very talented. We have found that if she is able to stay on site here with some of her peers, she can fix the problem faster. I suggest we arrange a video-conference call instead.
I want the COO (or other executive) to get on the phone.	Unfortunately the COO is traveling. What I suggest is we pull in the head of X technology. He really knows his stuff, and can likely give you the best information about this service outage.

Common Request	Gentle "No" Or More Time Response
I expect a X$$ credit as a result of this issue. We have lost a lot of business due to your outage.	I understand. After we hang up, I am going to immediately pull your contract and review it with our account team. Can we set up a follow-up call for this afternoon?
I need proof that the system is working at the contracted speed and volume per hour, so send me copies of all of your log files.	We want to meet, or exceed those speed and volume commitments. For information security and privacy reasons, I can not send you our log files. What I can do is set up a Webex and show you the log files for your company's installation of our product.

Chapter 13

The Mediums for Your Messages

The following communication tips could be applied to most business correspondence but are especially important when interacting with customers or asking for help internally.

More Discussion, Less Email

In many companies we tend to rely too much on email to communicate and help solve problems. Email is a good tool for a "first" interaction, or for a written summary after the fact. However, email is not the right tool when working back and forth with a customer or group of coworkers to solve difficult problems or to diffuse escalations.

Hard To Listen: Throughout this book, I have reinforced how important it is to listen to others when solving problems and resolving escalations. Emails are statements, not conversations. There is no way to practice active and timely listening via email.

Email adds time to resolution: I would guess that wasting time with email chains, can at least double the time it takes to get to the next step in problem resolution. Instead, get the right parties together on the phone, face to face, or some combination of both to talk through the issues at hand. As a leader, if you start to get ccd on a back and forth email chain, step in and ask the team members to take the conversation offline.

Email is not emotional: Email can tell a factual story, but is not a medium to empathize or sympathize. Email is not a medium to have an emotional interaction, and all escalations are emotional. When you read email you cannot hear the support or frustration, you cannot see any facial impressions, and you cannot hear a tone of voice. Conversely, I have observed people incorrectly reacting to an email, because a word had capital letters, the email was too short or the email was too long. Email (and text messages) may add fuel to a fire, due to their impersonal nature.

Email is a permanent record and may include company confidential data and information. Email can be easily forwarded to employees within and external to an organization. With that in mind, the recipients should only be those who "need to know".

Online Tools

There are times when you need to communicate with a group of decision makers or a group of customers and have visual aids in addition to verbal updates. In these cases, leverage an online meeting tool such as Webex or Zoom. Using the embedded video tool will give you the ability to have some face to face contact and make the conversation more personal.

Wisely Invest in Face to Face

When dealing with complex problems, it is sometimes necessary to see the issues first hand or to work with a customer in a more hand's on, "show them how" manner. I have often heard the value of "breaking bread" with customers to strengthen a relationship and build trust, so that working together to solve problems becomes easier.

Before approving travel, be sure you understand the costs and benefits, and whether video conferencing or screen sharing may be a first alternative. There are some situations where the face to face time is definitely the best option.

Chapter 14

Keeping the C Levels Informed

In addition to effectively managing your customer communications, a well designed escalation process also governs activities that happen within your business. These include communications and work hand-offs from team to team, department to department, and to executives and C-Level staff.

Internal Update Template

There will be times that you must communicate the details of a customer escalation to other people across your business. When you craft these communications, it's important to remember that the recipients have (most likely) not been personally involved, are busy and are likely managing other business priorities. Also, depending on the role of the recipients, they may need more or less information.

I recommend that any internal communication about a customer escalation is brief, and has four main parts. These are a summary, the actions, the root cause and the next steps.

1) Summary: The first part of the message is a level setting summary. It should include a high level description of the situation and the purpose of the communication. The purpose could be for awareness, to ask for help or to motivate action.

2) Actions: The second part is a summary of the actions taken to date to diagnose and resolve the customer's issue. Bullet points are a good method to share this information.

3) Root Cause: Part three should describe the why behind the customer's problem. If it is yet to be determined, include the current hypotheses and a date for when the root cause will be found.

4) Next Steps: The final section should clearly describe the next steps with target completion dates and owners.

Sample Communication

Here is a sample, internal communication for a hypothetical escalation with Xtra Retail Shops.

Summary:

For awareness only: Xtra Retail Shops, our largest North America retail account, experienced a 1 hour product outage today, June 25, from 8AM to 9AM. Their assigned Account Executive, Todd Smith, and the VP of Support, Susan Mitchell, met at noon with their CIO and CEO. Customer is most concerned with permanent remediation of root cause for their on-premise accounting software prior to July 4 holiday.

Key Actions To Date:
- 8 AM: Xtra Retail CIO escalated to Todd Smith directly to report outage.
- 8:15 AM to 8:40 AM: Our Accounting Software technical team met with Xtra's technical team to diagnose the issue.
- 8:40 AM to 8:50 AM: Technical team identified workaround fix.
- 8:55 AM: Customer implemented workaround fix and within 5 minutes regained service.

Root Cause:
- A software code defect was found in the historical processing module. This was part of 6.0 release deployed week of June 3.

Next Steps:
- Shelley Franks, VP of Engineering, will work with her staff and Xtra's technical team to further review code defect and create and test code fix, by July 1.
- Todd Smith and Susan Mitchell will hold daily update calls with customer at 8AM and 4PM ET to provide status updates.
- Susan Mitchell will coordinate code deployment with customer by the morning of July 3.

We have all critical resources working on this issue. Please contact me with any questions. I will provide an update to this distribution in 24 hours.

- Marci Reynolds

Adjust The Message To The Audience

As a general rule, senior executives want to hear or read a summary of the issue, know the causes, and most important, what the next steps are and who owns the resolution. Conversely, a technical audience may want to get into the deep details of an issue including technical jargon, error messages etc. Adjust the messages accordingly.

In addition, if you need help solving the problem or remediating the escalation, limit the audience of your communication to the critical few, who can actually help you. Be clear in what kind of help you need, from whom and by when. Make sure the recipients understand the criticality of the issue and the impact of not taking any action.

Timing

Email used to be considered fast, but now we live in a world of instant messaging, texting and tweeting. When you are faced with a very serious customer issue and escalation, I recommend sending a text message to the key internal employees who need to know, even before the issue is resolved.

In my most recent role, I would ping my boss, the head of engineering, the head of technical support and occasionally the COO, with a quick text as soon as I was aware of an issue. It could be something as simple as, "Head's up- Xtra Retail in midst of outage. All hands on deck. More info shortly".

Chapter 15

How to Leverage Internal Escalation Paths

Have you ever seen an internal escalation email that is sent to the entire world? The email may have included you, your boss, your boss's boss, the head of technology, the janitor, the cook and even your mother. These types of communication often happen when employees do not know the proper method to escalate issues.

Know the path: Document clear escalation paths for the most common types of issues. For example, when issue A happens, then your first contact is to manager Fred Smith. If Fred is unavailable, contact director Sandra Harrington. If Sandra is not available, then contact vice president Wendy Rodriguez.

Know the medium: Determine the best method(s) to escalate within your business. For example, for certain types of issues, you may agree to start with an email communication. For more serious issues, you may determine that a conference call is more valuable.

In my experience, the more people you add to an internal escalation update or ask for help, the slower you will resolve the issue. Extra people tend to cause noise in the process. Limit the audience of any escalation communication to the critical few, who need to know and/or can actually help you.

Senior Leadership Involvement

In 2017, KPMG Consulting published an outstanding white paper titled, "B2B Customer Experience: Winning in the Moments that Matter". In addition to providing some excellent insights across the end to end experience matrix, KPMG also incorporated recommendations related to the handling of service failures and escalations.

One specific area of guidance focused on the involvement of Senior Leadership in critical escalations. Specifically, this study reinforced that customers expect senior people to be visible, not invisible when things get difficult.

This is not possible for every customer, but should be a best practice and standard with your top customers.

This could be as simple as a senior leader sending a quick note to a key decision maker saying, "I am aware of your service challenges and I am making sure we have our top people working to resolve it as soon as possible". Or, it could take the form of a phone call or meeting.

With that said, senior leaders can listen and assist, but normally do not have the experience to remediate a complex issue.

When a customer escalation comes to me in an executive role, my focus is on listening to the customer and really understanding what happened. While we talk, I take lots of notes, and there is always one thing in common at the end of our conversations. That is, I am usually not the person who can actually help the customer with their problem. Why? Because I am not close enough to their work and do not have the right level of subject matter expertise.

Interestingly, there is often a trend when I follow-up with the team's that are/were doing the work for the customer. The team members involved know there are problems. They have been working really hard, sometimes 24/7 to solve the complications. They really care about the customer, but they have not yet been successful. Even with these challenges there is often a hesitation to escalate or ask for more help internally.

As mentioned in Chapter 9, create an environment where employees are not afraid to ask for help, and leverage the "good" kind of escalations.

Avoid Skip Level Escalations

A skip level escalation occurs when a problem is not brought directly to a leader's attention and is instead brought to his or her boss's boss or even higher in an organization.

What happens when you skip levels in a business environment? Usually nothing very productive. It leads to long email chains, urgent requests, drop everything meetings, bruised egos and stress. It may spur some action for the issue, but there are much better ways to approach this.

Ideally, you should escalate by following a defined path. In lieu of a defined path, escalate to the team that is closest to the work and or the direct manager of that team, before escalating higher.

One caveat to the skip level advice is regarding "head's up " emails. Sometimes it is wise to notify a senior leader when large issues are being addressed, to keep them in the loop and avoid future surprises. Be sure that they know you have everything under control and that the purpose of the communication is awareness only.

Chapter 16

The Importance of Follow-up

After you successfully resolve a customer escalation, there is one more step left, which is following up. This includes following up with the customer, with any employees who were involved and with any C-level executives who were notified. Following up is the icing on the escalation cake!

External Follow-up

As mentioned earlier, studies have shown that when a customer has a problem and they perceive that the supplier effectively resolves the problem, they tend to spend more, be more loyal and are more likely to recommend that supplier. Following up with your customer is your opportunity to check in and confirm that the customer is satisfied, and to handle any loose ends that may be remaining. It is also a chance to show that you care and to deepen the customer relationship.

Internal Follow-up

It is common that cross-functional employees will help you identify, manage and resolve customer escalations. Take the time to say thank you and to recognize the employees who made things happen. This could be as simple as sending a brief email, making a phone call or leveraging a company's internal rewards systems. Saying thank you will help boost employee morale and engagement.

If a problem is serious enough that you had to notify C-level executives, then it is serious enough for a follow-up note. Shortly after the escalation is resolved, send a quick email summary of the activities to those who were previously notified.

The note should reinforce that the problem is now resolved, should describe the current satisfaction level of the customer (often called the temperature, i.e. red, yellow or green) and should recap any next steps that are planned in coming weeks or months. Sending this follow-up note is a great way to demonstrate leadership and bring closure to an event.

Chapter 17

Assess Your Escalation Management Approach

By now you are pumped up and ready to improve your escalation management program, right?! Here are some questions to discuss with your boss or your team, to determine your escalation management readiness. I recommend that you go through this list and then put together an action plan for improvement based on the information you collect. (To assist with these efforts, I have included two, quick-reference guides in the Appendix following this chapter.)

- **Inspect expectations:** Are customer offerings clearly documented and offered? Are unclear customer expectations leading to future escalations? What behavior do we need to start or stop? Are we over promising or providing incorrect information?

- **Understand:** What are the primary reasons that customers escalate? What early warning systems are in place to allow staff members to take action, before an escalation happens?

- **Empower:** How have you empowered the front line employees to resolve the majority of issues before asking for approval from others? Do employees understand they are the primary point of contact or are they handing-off problems to other departments? Are your approval workflows only focused on the exceptions? Do employees feel comfortable asking for help?

- **Prioritize**: What are the criteria for your top customer list? Where is the top customer list stored and how often is it updated. Do employees know how a top customer should be treated, versus a "regular" customer?

- **Converse:** What are the best practices for responding to the most common customer requests? Do customer facing employees understand how to use positive language, even when saying no? What has your company agreed on in terms of the right time for using email, holding meetings or traveling on site, when addressing escalations?

- **Update:** When and for what types of issues, should internal employees provide updates on escalations to upper management? How frequently should they provide updates? Is this workflow documented and communicated across the organization? Do employees know when to follow-up with customers after an escalation has been resolved.

I wish you great success with your escalation management program!

Appendix

Customer Lifecycle Steps That Could Lead To Escalations

Step in Customer Lifecycle	Task	Notes on Readiness
Presales - Sales	Clearly document customer offerings including product, price timing. Include in contract.	
	Clearly document customer expectations. Include in contract. Define the role they play in the successful product or service.	
	Train sales team on both company offerings and customer expectations.	
Implementation Onboarding	Clearly document, gain agreement on and communicate project schedules.	
	Provide consistent updates internally and externally.	

Step in Customer Lifecycle	Task	Notes on Readiness
	Hold internal and external resources accountable for meeting project goals and timelines.	
Post-Implementation Ongoing Support	Train support team on both company offerings and customer expectations.	
	Coach and empower support team members to make the majority of decisions on behalf of the customers.	
	Focus decision approval workflows on exceptions only.	
	Leverage people, process and technology to understand why and when customers escalate.	
	Implement early warning systems to prevent escalations.	
	Identify, document and share Top Customer List.	

How To Reduce Customer Escalations
Quick Reference sheet

Contributors

Michael Pace, Principal at The Pace Of Service, Customer Experience consulting. President and Board Member of NorthEast Contact Center Forum www.neccf.org, @micpace

Carolyn Urban, VP Customer Services, www.carbonblack.com

Sources

Beaujean, M (2016, February) The moment of truth in customer service, from https://www.mckinsey.com

CCMC Consulting, (2017) 2017 Customer Rage Study, from https://www.customercaremc.com/

C-Cubes Consulting, (2017) C-CUBESTM B2B Benchmark 2017, PDF, from http://ccubes.net

Chambers, Sarah, (2020, February 14) 9 Real World Examples of Setting Clear Expectations with Your Customers, https://www.nicereply.com/blog/setting-customer-expectations/

Circle Research, (Date not shown. Retrieved 2018, November) B2B Customer Satisfaction White Paper, from https://www.circle-research.com

CSSP (Date not shown. Retrieved 2018, November) Customer satisfaction, what research tells us, from https://cssp.org/publications-resources/

Dimensional Research (2013, April) Customer service and business results: A survey of customer service from mid-size companies, from https://d16cvnquvjw7pr.cloudfront.net

Filek, J. (2010, Feb 1) Top reasons calls get escalated, from https://www.impactcommunicationsinc.com/

Gartner (2018, July 30), Gartner Says Customer Experience Pyramid Drives Loyalty, Satisfaction and Advocacy, from https://www.businesswire.com/

Hyken, Shep (2019, December), Customer Service and CX Predictions for 2020, Forbes, from https://www.forbes.com/sites/shephyken/2019/12/22/customer-service-and-cx-predictions-for-2020/#7145a2b27f6f

Islam, Gareen, "2019 Customer Expectations Report, Gladly, from https://www.gladly.com/latest/2019-customer-expectations-report/

Kalb, I (2011, June 23) How customer complaints can improve business, from https://www.cbsnews.com

Larons, J, (2018, July 19) How to handle customer complaints to build better loyalty, from https://blog.hubspot.com/

Maechler N, (2016, March) Improving the business to business customer experience, from https://www.mckinsey.com

Mills, D (2017, March 14) In 2020 customer experience will overtake price and product quality as key differentiator, from https://www.jacada.com/

Patel, N (Date not shown. Retrieved 2018, November) 5 ways to turn your unhappy customers into a resources, from https://neilpatel.com/

Qualtrics, (2015 to 2018) blog and news articles, https://experiencematters.blog/

Qualtrics, (2019) ROI of Customer Experience Study, https://www.qualtrics.com/xm-institute/roi-of-customer-experience-2019/

The Ritz Carlton Leadership Center (2015, October 7) Dos and Dont's of setting customer expectations, from http://ritzcarltonleadershipcenter.com

Totango, (2016, July 18) Understanding Early Warning Systems for Customer Success, from https://blog.totango.com/2016/07/understanding-early-warning-systems-for-customer-success/

Walker International, (Date not shown. Retrieved 2018, November) Customers 2020, the future of B2B customer experience, white paper, from https://www.walkerinfo.com/

About the Author

Marci Reynolds is a customer operations expert with deep expertise in leading business to business, customer support, customer experience strategy and service delivery functions. She has led global teams up to 600 people, supporting mission critical products and services, 24/7/365.

Most recently, Marci was the Executive Vice President of Customer Delivery for ACI Worldwide, a leading, payments software company. Marci spent more than eight years with ACI in leadership positions of increasing responsibility. Prior to ACI, she held customer operations leadership roles at Monster.com, Deluxe Corporation, Staples and The Boston Globe.

She has her Master's Degree in Business & Operations from Bentley University, and a Bachelor's Degree in Business Administration from Northeastern University.

Marci is originally from Boston, Massachusetts, and currently resides with her family in the Atlanta, Georgia area. When she is not leading teams or business writing, she enjoys volunteering for animal rescue organizations, and teaching yoga.

Content

Copyright 2020. All rights to this content are reserved. Content may quoted only with appropriate attribution to author, Marci Reynolds. Marci can be reached by emailing her at marcireynolds@comcast.net.

www.ingramcontent.com/pod-product-compliance
Lightning Source LLC
Chambersburg PA
CBHW071121240526
45465CB00022B/743